Also by Jack Ramey

The Future Past

Death Sings in the Choir of Light

Burnt Almonds

Eurydice's Kiss

Turtle Island: A Dream of Peace

Eavesdropping in Plato's Cafe

EAVESDROPPING IN PLATO's CAFÉ

Jack Ramey

Springwood
PRESS

First Edition

Copyright © 2015 by Jack Ramey

Library of Congress Control Number: 2015934923

ISBN 978-1-943112-78-4

Printed in the United States of America

All rights reserved.
For permission to reproduce selections
from this book, please contact:

Springwood Press, LLC
302 Fairmount Drive
Madison IN 47250

springwoodpress.org

for Nancy

Change is my theme. You gods, whose power has
wrought all transformations, aid the poet's thought,
And make my song's unbroken sequence flow
From earth's beginnings to the days we know.

— Ovid

Contents

World–Soul

Another Day in Paradise	3
The Spiral Destiny	6
Vanity, All is Vanity	8
Earth Day	10
Glad Day	11
Mother's Day	12
A Wish	14
Meditation 9	15
All Creatures Great and Small	16
Ode to the Tao in Winter	18
Resurrection and Ascension	20
One Easter Sunday	22
One More Time	23
The Light from their Eyes	24
Wind in Autumn	26
The Widowed Fields	27
Morning Snowfall Sutra	28

Ghost-Dance

Nineteen Lines for the Czarina's Children	31
Kali Yuga	32
Fragments from the Gone World	34
Ghost Road	48
Event Horizon	49
Crow Poem	50
Eavesdropping in Plato's Café	51
Prologue as the Curtain Rises	51
Act I	52
Act II	64
The Discourse of the Ashtrays	66
Act III	70

End-Games

The Angel of Time	81
To Age Slowly Without Pain	82
Two Hundred and Six Bones	84
Through a Glass Darkly	86
Memento Mori	88
Prisoner of Hope	89
Song of Gog	90
The Psychic Torment of Dreams	96
Lines for the End of the Mayan Calendar	98
Freedom Day	100
Gun	102
Fandango	103
Poem at the End of a Deadly Year	104
Gabriel's Horn	106
Desideratum	107

World-Soul

Another Day in Paradise

The idle rusticity of spring
in her green languor,
the abundance of her,
the sweet charm of her laughter

echoes down through
my network of nerves coiled
out through my spine
to thrill the cobra root of my soul.

Fine the ballet dance of five
white butterflies above clover,
fine the flash of a robin's breast
as he fights off a challenger

to his domain, his patch
of wormy soil, his meal ticket
for his mate and younglings
beneath a lush thicket of brush.

The heartbeat tick of a clock
in the lull between bird call
and thrilling song
chills the mind reminded of the Final

Conductor's railroad call:
this is your own ticket to ride
the one-way railway to forever,
the Sunset Limited's tidal

stop at the Delta, spreading out
her cars in shirring motion,
fanning out across the gulf
between us and that far off ocean

of never-ending sleep.
The fractal logic of a maple leaf
gentling moving at branch's end,
repeating the pattern of each

of her neighbors, but each one
slightly different, each one
a green sibling to the others
telepathically talking of the sun's

generous photosynthesis reaching
up and down through
branch after antlered branch
down to her limbs' heartwood to

the kundalini of her sappy spine
that sings out praises and charms
to spring, matching the beat of wings
that come to rest in her arms.

The green of it all from lawn to
canopy of tree calls out to my very
life's blood flooding through
my heart up to my brain weary with

postmodern tedium and rush,
the ennui of too much information
like plants from another planet
who wrap their hungry tendril tongues

around you, surround you,
choke you until there is nothing left
but a dry husk emptied out,
head full of useless trivia about theft

or murder or everlasting war
between everlasting warring factions on TV

in the movies in newspapers
on the internet's vast distraction machine.

Oh green paradise lost in the sterile
minimalism of techno-oppression:
bring back to me the fragile logic
of your mystery veiled by Maya's marathon

dissemination running always
to torment the psyche, the soul, the spirit
longing for the peace of deep
vertical thought and meditation fraught

with Spanish waves of taut inquisition.
Let us sit then beneath a willow tree
Buddha tree beside a goldfish pond
surrounded by bees and flowers dreaming

away the day as if it were the strings
of an instrument tuned in heaven
fretting out the notes of joy and bliss
writ on vellum in ancient notation

hugged by a passion felt deep down
to the core of creation's volcanic roar
lifting the thrilling heart above the turmoil,
startled by a glimpse of forever

always and ever and anon rolling on
and on and on until something stops you
and you are hurled back upon
the ground panting, sweating, face lifted up to

the sky through grass and leaves
like the face of Bernini's Saint Teresa ecstatic in
afterglow, laid low beneath cupid's arrow,
ravished by God's holy communion.

The Spiral Destiny

Look at the light beams
pouring down from the sun:–
slicing through morning fog
and mist like a million surgeons'

carefully sharpened knives
in a medieval cathedral of medicine,
where patients wait patiently,
supine on the mossy floor of love

in the nave of, in the name of,
the greater synagogue of creation.
Just look at the dew-strewn leaves
and petals gleaming through mist:–

up-turned lips waiting to be touched
by Dawn's rosy-fingered first
caress not unlike those aforementioned
metaphorical patients floored

by the glory of their great mother's
lovely smile after two days
of her tears, gray rain
nourishing the roots of their being, crying

down on her children her lachrymose blessing,
her forgiveness for
those who hurt her daily
with chemical needles and warlike drones

that daily rain down their own brutal
tears on her innocent body
and the bodies of children
who one day may just stop, who already

seem to have stopped evolving
toward some greater understanding.
Look at the river valley still hugged
in fluff, puffed up with cloudy stuff

masking the flow of her borderless destiny,
her spiral world without
beginning or ending, her always
striving movement toward the sea.

Vanity, All Is Vanity

Sometimes
I want to be like Wang Wei
or any other Chinese poet
silent on a cold mountain top

looking down on corrupt
civilization and the brutality
of all species struggling to live
out their days feeding on others.

Sometimes
I want to be like Bruce Wayne
with a dark secret identity
using my mind and pop-techno-toys
to fight evil and crime.

But what is evil? And who
decides what acts are crimes?
The hive-mind? Or the unseen
rulers of the world who have
held us all in thrall for centuries?

Sometimes
I want to be like Jesus
walking sandaled across the land
healing the sick and raising the dead
but then again I do not want to die hanging

on a cross after flogging and torture
and all your friends deserting you
because they do not want to die like you.

Sometimes
I want to be like Orpheus or Saint Francis
with birds landing all over my head
and shoulders and fingers and arms
all the dark gentle creatures
of the forest come around to talk to me,

to walk with me as I tell them
about the joys of poetry
and meditation, the devotion
of ecstasy and rapture – things that they
actually already know in their furry
feathered minds, and they then teach me

how to be in the world,
simple and holy and pure,
without wanting to be someone else.

Earth Day

The sun this morning makes
all things bright with Apollonian light :

crocus, redbuds, wild violets,
magnolia blossoms perfuming the air.

Everywhere, colors gleam off retinae
of creatures high and creatures low :

angels and insects, demons and beasts,
women and men, the fractal eye of a butterfly,

wings dandelion-gold flashing by the ink-spot eye
of a wary dove, the yellow eye of a stalking cat :

all alive, all born again of earth this magic spring
in the waning career of a choking, spinning planet.

Glad Day – March 21st

The Sun ladles out his clarity
with such dollops of munificence.

Snows melt into ground, warming,
and it seems as if Spring crawls apace

and the earth is blessed
with the grace of renewal:

the great creative powers dormant,
captive in tree-sap and bulb-root

breathing in dirt and breathing in me
all stirred up by this great cosmic charity.

Mother's Day

False dawn 6 a.m.
five or six birds chirp up the sun
which does not rise
so much as glower through
the gray rain.

It is Mother's Day
in the USA
and the true Mother
of us all is sodden,
crying for her wayward

children here on
the bloody banks
of the Ohio
cutting its way through
southern Indiana

toward some
eventual destiny we
are not privy to. We do
know technologically
speaking she flows

to Cairo Illinois
to join the Mississippi
and then down to New
Orleans to fan out
across the oily Gulf.

But what is this
deadly gulf really?

Is it metaphor for
some eternal vision
of God's grandeur,

His distance between
us and other galaxies
whose stars are the vellum
His true poem is writ upon?
Is it the true Mother's

affidavit that states
that no matter what
man does to her or
himself she will survive,
she will outlive all extinct

species to heal her state
and create more? Brave
but too many questions
hurt the mind that aches
for precise clarity

on this rainy Sunday
Mother's Day
tucked inside the strange
theology we humans
have created, debated,

and killed for, over
centuries of uncivil
obedience to too many
laws we have created to
explain this fragile mystery.

A Wish

Sunshine, tea, and negative capability.
The morning quakes with possibility
on fire with desire to create, to make
sense and spirit from nothingness,
to reach for the sublime, hidden within
the silken folds of mystery and wonder,
tear aside the seven veils of illusion
and hold it in the palm of your hand
like a trembling bird not of this earth,
not asking to understand, not demanding
proof, only the player's request: a chance.

Meditation 9

Zazen on a zafu
on a zabuton
in the zendo
of fragile existence.
What am I doing here?
Here on this atom
spinning in infinite space
with billions of other
aimless creatures pondering
the same question
or dully wandering along
the same repetitive pathways
their forbears trod
in ignorance ages ago.
Just a speck, a mote
floating in the eternal
shaft of light whose
source is hidden
from our view behind
half-opened venetian blinds
pulled by a hand
that is not a hand
that is an odorless essence
beyond our understanding.
Zazen on a zafu
on a zabuton
in the zendo
of ultimate existence.

All Creatures Great and Small

1

Picking up a stone
this morning
the size of my palm
a hundred or so micro-
ants scurry in deliberate
frenzy to protect their young
larvae scrambling onto
my hand.

I smash two
between thumb and finger
as easy as breathing.
Casual. Unthinking. Unfeeling.
Their lives' meaning
mean nothing to me.

As I am to these small
creatures, these nano-ants,
so the universe of gods is to me.
As I am to the humble bee
buzzing around me,
so wingèd spirits are to me:–
they hover above and around me,
surround me with veils of mystery
that hedge me, send me pledges
of security in this dale of uncertainty.

2

Spring rain soft down in the morning
gentle cleansing weather
in April's calm false spring;

my mind is labyrinthine—woods
tangled with vines, brambles,
nettles, burrs, and vast fields of

sleeping flowers: bulbs beneath
the surface that will one by one
spear through the trepanned earth

like crocus buds :
open up, bloom, and pass away
again until next year :

they are the transmigration of souls
perennially reincarnating themselves
like thought and divine imagination.

Ode to the Tao in Winter

The overture to Rossini's Semiramide
galloping in my ears and periodically
punching me upside my head
while the sky's on fire beside me
as I race down the highway at speeds
unimaginable in the nineteenth century.

The clouds' gray calligraphy
spells out the Tao before me:
> *Best to be like water,*
> > *Which benefits the ten thousand things*
> > *And does not contend.*

Run silent; run deep; be still like a wood-
land pool in winter mantled with layers of ice
wherein golden leaves are captured, still
with the dead and deathless chill of grace.

Be a bridge between heaven and earth,
sky and mud, what is in and what is out,
not like prophets of a vengeful jealous god
but a conduit for the creative force of the universe:
the Father-Mother, the One who dwells in love.

> *Favor and disgrace are like fear.*
> *Honor and distress are like the self.*
> *Respect the world as your self:*
> > *The world is your lodging.*
> *Love the world as your self:*
> > *The world can be your trust.*

Let me embrace the joy of my life
without anger, without fear, without worry,

and live most fully in the ancient Tao,
master the existing present
understand the source of all things
be one with stone, with grass, with tree
with sun and moon and cloud, with river
until my span has spun out at last its golden thread
and the Fates cast it free with their mystic scissors.

Resurrection and Ascension
After reading the morning news

Such properties as these do make me funk.
I shall go outside and become one with ducks,

who must for now remain invisible,
even though they seem indivisible

from my poor twisted psyche today
in a world full of grand plans and final disarray.

The drama and dharma of the purple iris
petal, and the innocence of the wild daisy's kiss

all attest to this: there is a power deep down things
a leafy testament from grass to trunk to bird wings

lighting on branch tips swinging in the breeze
of spring's morning lifting light alike to ants and me

and all of creation. A rare honey bee at my window
becomes an ageless Blakean angel reborn in aura-glow

of all seven colors of chakra's rainbow :
her buzz a mantra hymn to what is holy now

and always will remain so: the tidal flow
of connected electrons that spin and show

how vital and how sacral is the soul of earth
the grand cycle of birth and life and death

here on this plane of existence where we
wrestle with sorrow and joy, doubt and belief.

Are we really here on this struggling planet or
do we dream this brief butterfly dream for

only a moment, mate then with the pleading
cry of our mother; die, and rise up again, bleeding,

whole and free? Will we discover a new creed,
a covenant covered in green leaves that breed

forth regeneration, resurgent song sprung from
the great well of divine imagination spun from

the words and mind of the holy multiverse that dives
and swims through all planes of existence, thrives

on the blood of the poet, the aura of angels, the high
and low call of all thrumming, humming, trumpeting life

seen in the heart of a flower, the vein of a leaf,
the blood-filled arteries in lungs that breathe with the beat

and pulse of the heart of the stars, fire of our godlike sun,
our goddess moon that shine down their brilliant sum

of enlightenment upon our heads, ready to wed, to meld
with earth, with air, with water, with all things living, cold

with all things dead, in the mold of clay we are shaped with
in the crystalline air that is our stairway that we escape with :

one at last with the encompassing matrix of existence.

One Easter Sunday

Soft weather the end of March
the sky is eggshell, the river gray.

A soft rain lightly jewels rocks and trees
and the fox and the deer walk freely

among the rising purple crocus, the yellowing
jonquils, eating calmly what they please.

They do not speak of God and dogma
or how this day God's Son is risen

up from the grave in robes of purple
to save creation from death and sin.

They know no death or sin.
They know only life and love

each second burning wholly within them.
They know no god but the one that runs

along the paths of their blood :
the immaculate soul of Deer God

breathing like heart-prayer through their veins
beating like bird-cry above their six and holy senses.

Fox God whose sharp teeth shine in the sun
whose hunting heart bursts apart with joy

and the souls of all the small creatures in the field
below me cry out in ecstasy: life! life! the miracle

bared again each annual spin of the earth, oh rare
sacred oneness, oh precious genesis again.

One More Time

Thirteen and twa more children
taught me how to sing and pray
down here in Brazzaville.
Down in the alleys away from the shore
where stray dogs chase gray rats
and lost ones toss happy dice
for the land that has turned hostile
against them – insect tribes and nations
rising up relentless against those
who would keep them down
sucking blood and sap from
hosts whose flesh and bark
is easy prey. How can you fight
what you cannot see? After a stroll
across that pleasant meadow
parasites lodge themselves ruthlessly
persistently, pitilessly, and will not give up
until you weaken and die and your tribe
becomes extinct, an afterthought,
and Jesus will come back as a mantis
to rule over the New Kingdom of the earth.

The Light from Their Eyes

They come after dark to eat wheat grass
when they know no crossbow will target them :

a freeway of eyes flashing like headlamps
on bright from the beam of my flashlight

shining from high above them on my deck as I grill
steaks from the tender loin of a deer I recently killed.

All I can see is the light that shines from their eyes
like silver discs that lead down to doe-and-fawn soul,

the *ki* alive in them as they stand frozen
staring at this dim mini-mag-beam as if it were

some pale ghastly reflection of a moonbow
or a shallow ghost of the sun haunting them,

chasing them through fog and shadow.
One bows low her head nodding up and down,

asking the eternal question: *Whose?* The same dread
question Whitman asked of the child's handful of leaves,

of the dropped handkerchief's owner. Slowly
they move and I can almost see their stately legs

and long ears like the dim outline of the dark moon
when the new moon has her charmed in her arms,

but it's the eyes, the luminous eyes that glow quick
like moonstones in a pagan idol's head hid in a cave,

on an ancient continent, and suddenly unearthed
to speak a lost tongue, a forgotten language of thought.

Wind in Autumn

Contrails' pretty poison quickly
shifts east by west wind's breath

in straight white diagonal arrows
high above my head. The dime-sized

jet liner like the leaden echo of Diana's bow
or Apollo's own halo worn slant and low on his brow.

Everywhere babies are being born early or late
on straw mats in huts or staph-laced sheets on hospital beds

while old ones lay dying in delirious bliss
or the cold agony of fatal recognition, alone, always alone.

The sun slants through the gray
to brighten burnished trees yellow and golden

that sway, wildly loosing like dread
locks their leaves to the loco-motovating air

roaring like some invisible runaway freight train
while willows bend, extend their arms horizontal

in orison to the breath of the One, the Father-Mother
of inspiration whose words whisper through their leaves.

The Widowed Fields

The widowed fields
seen through windows
are winnowed over now :
combed through, bereft of fruitfulness,
harrowed out of all life above ground.

Now as the season of the witch
approaches, trailing darkness
in her wake, I awaken to such trite
reconnaissance as this: all things ripen and fall
in the great and golden time allowed us all.

Morning Snowfall Sutra

The snow flew all night long
making the morning white
and I arose like a child in winter
full of the purity and joy for
this cleansing act of nature.

The lone cedar tree, Shaman Tree,
leaning, her sibylline red arms
green boughs outstretched in orant pose
hands and head covered in snow,
beckons the morning's blessings

and I feel the ease of breath
from throat to heart,
hear the swift anima spiritus
streaming out from white fingers
of trees to reach my spirit,

my mind at peace, at one
with bird wing, hawk's eye
flying through green-temple space
heart singing with flower stalks
now covered in snow, gold
souls waiting for a new beginning.

Ghost-Dance

Nineteen Lines for the Czarina's Children

Like the small white ball in Delmore Schwartz's poem
that bounces out of the gilt room in the palace
and into infinity, lost, utterly lost
in the maelstrom of nothingness
so we too must bound out one day which day we know not

and rebound somewhere else somewhere unknown
where curious birds sing in unfamiliar plumage
a song unheard of in this life or any other life:
perhaps a sweet sound, perhaps a bitter one,
perhaps a sound that is impossible to hear

with human ears. When we get there we will have forgotten
all about the small white ball that once we were upon a time
we will have forgotten all but the moment of inbreath
and outstretch, a vast collapsing and expanding as if we were

the huge lungs of the universe,
a bellows as large as God's mythic mind
that thinks only in the present: no past no future
for these are concepts that do not exist in that far off place
only the everlasting constantly expanding second of now.

Kali Yuga

On cracked ancient krater
painted red, men black-
bearded wrestle,
hoist spear and penis
or recline in drapery
drinking wine
from shallow cups

restating thus this vessel's
earthly purpose. Keats' purple
bubbles winking at the brim
and yes they are all
fixed in, forever slim
forever holding the same positions;

and yes the maidens always loath,
the runner always wins,
the wrestlers frozen along the rim,
the satyrs always priapic.

But what does it prove?
That art is eternal? Immutable?
Essential? Death
in the end does not conquer,
does not shatter?

A silver helmet found
at the bottom of a river,
beside rusted sword blades,

dog and horse bones,
human bones
dung-flesh and blood ghosted away

centuries ago. A warrior,
gore-hero buried here,
strong-blood-and-death lover,
ring-giver, sent to Odin
with his weapons
his torcs, his women,
his slaves, his beasts

in a savage age
not unlike our own :
the age of Kali Yuga,
the age we are trapped in
like still figures
on a painted vase.

And is this too Art?
Is this the stuff
mankind's dust is
son and father to?
Shards in time,
slime breaking down
to slime.

Fragments from the Gone World

I

The gods are far too literal minded :
Ithmonike of Pellene
                pregnant for three entire years
after imploring the god Asklepios at Epidaurus.
You silly woman, he said upon her return,
why did you not say
                you wanted to give birth?

II

Fingernail-clipping moon
Above dustbin horsetail cloud.

A small moth ascends
As day descends
                into darkness.

Dawn breaks
My heart
Apart. Opens
                up the night
Like a knife wound
Spilling red across the horizon.

III

Great Egyptian Ptah, lord of creation,
spoke out loud his green-skinned imagination :
and the universe hurled off his tongue into being.

IV

Rose taffeta unwinds
from her spinning dancer's dress.

You've hurt me
for the last time, she says.

A rogue's gallery of blackguards
lines the walls of her memory

like a portico around her cerebellum's
cloister as baroque violoncellos squawk

in the nautilus hollows of her ears
like a dead sea of ancient tears.

You are gone now in dust
and I am still here, dancing.

V

Where neither rust nor moth consume
there must you find me
as I will find you.

We cannot escape our fate
as iron and wool cannot escape

the microscopic teeth of destiny
the microbial purge of decay.

VI

In Samarkand
did Tamburlaine

one hundred years
of war proclaim.
Mothers cursed his name
while Imams praised him.

Seventeen million souls
he sent to paradise or hell

while bringing Allah's word to
Asia's host of Buddhist infidels.

VII

Thor
loves a berserker
wild-eyed on mushrooms and mead:
shield in two pieces,
axe head bloody,
burning books he cannot read.

VIII

The ten eponymous heroes
of the ten tribes of Athens
squat on ten mounds of ashes
ten centuries deep.

IX

The blood sacrifice
of the Christ
is the sacrifice of
Mithras, of Osiris
of god-kings
who died that
their people might thrive
and who rose from the dead
to live forever.

X

The gods were first
men. Then
legends became
myth and myth
became religion.

XI

The sages said:
                "Seek the truth."
The truth will set you free.

But where now resides
the truth? Delphi
                no longer speaks.
Delos is silent.
Who now speaks
                truth to power
as Socrates did?

He died
>   by his own hand
>   >   at Athen's command:
his reward for seeking the truth.
And Howard Zinn is dead
>   and that smart device
that lurks
>   in your pocket or your purse
knows every move you make
on your journey to the Oracle of Google.

XII

Dionysus
was a god who could
take a joke.

In one of his plays
Aristophanes gave him
diarrhea in Hell

and the wine god
did not strike him dead
on the spot for blasphemy.

But, it is said,
Aristophanes later died of drink.

XIII

The Romans could not
subdue the Jews

so they destroyed them –
burned Jerusalem
                down to the ground
killed every man
woman and child
                that they found
wandering the olive-tree wasteland
or weeping in mud huts.
Except for the Sicarii,
those Dagger Assassins
who holed up at Masala.

They killed their own women
and children and then
                they killed themselves
down to the last man standing
who sliced through his own throat.

XIV

A monk rubs his tonsured head
and dips his brush
                in Northumbrian
hematite dust to paint a dragon's face
surrounding the holy *logos* of John.

Heathens pull their ships ashore
                and bang their axes
against the iron bosses of limewood shields.
The monk pauses, listening, his brush held
up, dripping red above the page.

XV

Imagine a planet
where mammoths
and bears outnumber people.

A mere ten thousand years ago
the human population of Earth
was five million bodies and souls.

You could fit them all
into two Toronto Canadas.

They were pretty much
the same as us
              except that the Sun
was their God
              and their timepiece;
the Moon was their Goddess
                  and calendar
and the revolution of the stars
was their constant tablet computer.

The water-waves in their bodies
lapped their bones like the tides of the sea
just like they do in you and me.

They had fire like us. They had knives
of flint and obsidian.
                    They knew well how to kill
sending arrows into beasts and men

stone hatchets into skulls :
                                   a great letting
of blood was always with them,
                                       caressing them.

The clever ones lived by rivers;
the dull ones lived by pain.

But they did not know yet
how to make crops rise up from the ground.

Ten thousand years ago
he or she who planted the first seeds
of wild rye or barley and reaped that first harvest
with jawbone sickle, started the leap
toward these nine billion twenty-first century souls.

XVI

Signs on leaves
hid in caves
loosed at last by wind.
The ten thousand shapes of death.

XVII

Marcus Crassus:
the richest man in Rome,
patron of Gaius Julius Caesar,
crucifier of Spartacus:

His head was used
as a prop in the final act
of *The Bacchae*
by an actor, Jason of Trolles,
to the great delight
of the Parthian king
at the wedding feast of his son.

XVIII

If it's not the objective
correlative, then
it's negative capability
or truth in beauty
or no ideas but in things
like wet wheelbarrows
or black boughs
or metaphors to live by
recollected in tranquility
or rebop beat sensibility.

But what about words?
Just words. The pure joy
and sacred vocation
of words, in a world tied
to image and icon like
packages in an endless aisle
stretching out to infinity
or bicameral eye in smartphones
held aloft by flying drones.

XIX

Truth: the jewel in the cave
hidden from sight :
numinous imminence
surrounding a cape worn by a saint,
but not just the opposite of lies :
lies contain their own kind of truth.

XX

I died at Antietam.
A minié ball shattered my spine.

Three ravens sat on my chest
and stared into my eyes
as I lay dying :

I entered this world blind,
eyeless in Elysium.

XXI

Louis Congo
they called me when I was alive,
my slave name – Louis for Louisiana,
Congo for where I was taken from.
Portuguese taught me to read and write
but sold me off to the Frenchman
who took me to New Orleans
when she was young in 1721.

Why they set me free to do their killing
I'll never know except they did not want
to do the deeds themselves I'll suppose.

Hung many a man both black and white,
broke their limbs on the wheel if need be;
flayed the skin from their backs if told to
with newly knotted cat o' nine tails.

This work got me my own house,
my own gal, and all the wine I could hold.
Now I am here with all the rest.

All them ghosts I sent before me
come to mock me every day
saying: No matter what you got,
no matter where you go,
no matter how well you lived,
we all end up in the same place.

XXII

Homer basked himself in Cretan sun :
the bright glare of light off the Mediterranean
flashed the pan of his retinal scan
blinding him while still young
but giving him Mnemosene's gift :
Memory. Plato's goddess
sent him succor, preserved thus
his lengthy line on down thru the ages
by sending him sages, singers
to keep his heroes alive
floating ceaselessly on the wine-dark sea.

XXIII

Beltane now :
the time of no-time
when the veil is thinned
and partly lifted
when the realm of faery
mingles with solid folk
when shape shifters, shadow
walkers float among us.

Sit beneath a tree
this night and you might see
the Faery Queen
riding her moon-white mare
but do not look at her
long unless you long to live
in the faery world forever.

XXIV

Bright Apollo
eternally young
    eternally new
leaps into his car each dawn
to guide his horses along
the rim of the sky's horizon.

Across the arc his horses run
tracing the clouds' azimuth
and the birds of air love him
and chant their praise and adoration.

Up higher his course He runs
bringing light and heat
to man and beast
woman and child
mortal and immortal,

But this is all as false
as false dawn is,
the astrophysicists are wont to say:
the Sun does not rise
                    or set
and the horizon is merely an illusion.

XXV

The winter trees, unmoored,
Float upward through the sky.

Gravity has failed them.
Tender fractals pierce

Waiting clouds, hungry and dry.

Magritte would be proud of them:
They remediate ramifications of his vision

As the woods fill up with snow
Again. The trees planted their seeds

In those clouds making them heavy
Giving birth to countless frozen stars

That startle the earth with brilliance
Floating up now and down then

Anchorless in the heaving sea of eternity.

XXVI

The huge eternal dark abyss
around which all galaxies
spin, circle, and slowly sink in
revolving, devolving, until after
billions of light years, they end up
one with the vast heavy nothing
or else become gateways to a new universe.

XXVII

Simonides of Keos
inventor of the art of memory
said that painting is silent poetry
and poetry is painting that speaks.

He knew the true poet's wish:
to make a poem whose images speak
to so many people that its words
live on forever.

                      But forever is much too long
a time. Just ask poor Sappho whose poems
cannot be found except in tiny scraps:
one stuck here, one stuck there,
one found wrapped around a mummy's head,
recycled to preserve a politician's memory.

Ghost Road

These passengers are always with me
On my journey down to the sea
Where sailboats list and bob endlessly by the quay.
I do not know them. They do not know me.
We ride together on melting roads each day.

Not speaking. Only sometimes to cry
Out warnings or exclaim aloud our dismay
At the mystery, the misery. Save us they seem to say.
I cannot save them and they
Cannot save me as we drive down broken highways
To reinvent the collapsing superstructure of our dreams.

Event Horizon

Psychotic dogs bark at cold winter stars,
chips of dead ice on the black painted canvas
of night. They sense the distance. The distance
between them and all other matter, the enormous
space between all living things: atoms, planets,
people, mountains, worms, moles, birds, gods, angels,
unspeakable stars burning in unknowable galaxies.
I hear the punition of bliss in endless, mindless meridian.

Crow Poem

A murder of crows flies over my head and settles in trees
beside my house of dark sonnets and unearthly dreams
deciding by my face that this is the place for them to be.

They think I'm a bird-happy sap and will not want
to kill them. They are right. Black as midnight's cat
and twice as smart, they remember Homer and Simonides

the poet who invented the Art of Memory in ancient Greece
over two thousand years ago. They speak in many
tongues, mimicking a baby's cry or the bleating of many sheep

or caw-cawing their raucous collective caw up through their craw
to signal the approach of hawk or eagle or human with gun.
Corax corax, given the gift of speech by the same Olympian gods

who bound Prometheus to a rock for bringing light to mortals
for usurping the task of divinity, prefiguring Lucifer, the bearer
of light, and by extension, darkness, dark as a crow's wing,

the favored writing instrument of countless playwrights
and poets and scribes in their monkish cowls patiently
copying out the texts of Matthew, Luke, Paul and John

the Revelator: dire prophecies and bright poesies flowing from
ink down through the veins in their sleek and hollow wing tips
onto parchment, scraped vellum, or Egyptian papyrus, and left

for us to wonder at, to ponder at, the dark mysteries of antiquity.

Eavesdropping in Plato's Café
A Metaphysical Polylogue

Prologue as the Curtain Rises

The great ones,
the sad and trapped ones,
cannot see us.
They exist in the ether,
taking endless whiskey or tea
over conversations that go on eternally.

We, the eavesdroppers, voyeurs,
see all, hear all,
fly to their tables
like sparrows after crumbs.

M. Plato,
great interlocutor
perpetual cross-examiner
owns and operates
this place.

His voice will often mingle
with those of his patrons.

All Western Philosophy
is a footnote to me,
he is fond of saying;
besides, I mix a mean martini.

Watch closely
listen not too literally
as, behind the curved bar,
in greasy leather apron
and robe, he
prepares,
metaphysically,
for another evening.

Act I

The Ideal Form of the shot glass
existing in
God's ontological eye, slant-wise
thru a lens not yet perfected on earth
neither convex, nor concave
fragmented and whole in a way
only an insect's eye can properly
perceive, but the way,
the rare way
light plays on its surface;
not the natural light, divine
light of the Sun, but the creeping
florescence born of a dumb mouther
of first principles
as I wipe
with my rag
the lipstick smudge
from its rim
and hold it up for inspection.

Then the bar stool, placed just so
her 4 legs pyramiding up to a
mimesis of a circle covered
in the tanned white hide of
oxen slain in Apollonian augury

upon whose copy
philosophers' butts are parked
on Friday nights
holding high converse
trapped here forever
circular anus
on circular form
xenophobic
xeroxes of themselves reborn
repeating the dialectic
they died with.

Take for example Nietzsche here
who never leaves this table, placed just so
in the corner
facing the wall where I have hung
Moreau's painting
solely for his entertainment;

it exists, you might say, as
his will-to-obsession.
Tolstoy and Arnold
bait him ceaselessly;
they fail to see
its perverse fascination
its eternal hold on Nietzsche's imagination.

(M. Plato wipes his hands
on his robe,
moves from behind the bar,
and does his slow deliberate shuffle
to Nietzsche's table.)

The usual, Herr Nietzsche?
Oui, Monsieur P. Do you see
how the hand of the androgyne
is placed just so? either sucking
out all the power of Apollo
or bestowing on his limp form
the strength and frenzied genius
of electric Dionysian force?

Plato rolls his eyes in the direction
of the painting (1893, a banner year
for perversity) a huge, nude semi-androgynous
creature, eyes fixed in hypnotic stare,
hair a mass of burning copper
cape of spongy organic matter
feet rooted deep in swamp
tendrils reaching toward sex
thighs entwined with green caress.
The mystic queen of chthonic darkness
king of death's decaying cave
towers above a dying
or enthralled Apollo
golden harp strapped to
his back, eyes closed, mouth in a moan
her huge hand toys with his crown
as he languishes in foetid bracken.

A strange man, Gustave Moreau, says
M. Plato as he does his slow peripatetic
arc to the bar to fetch Herr Nietzsche's drink.

Nietzsche's eyes glow in numinous rapture:
Lou, Lou, you were the garden in which, how
shall I say, all these old songs were sung,
you the touchstone, template for my weighty
armor, forge of my amour, a freight
I carried around like a fright
that worked its shamanistic cure
on my diseased imagination.
It was, finally, a chore, a burden,
the onerific stone of all those years
bore down and strangled my walk
until the garden path
became Golgotha's stations
my severed head adorned
your silver plate. . .

   Tolstoy joins Nietzsche
startling his reverie
lowering slowly his aristocratic peasant
bulk into the captain's chair
at the polyurethaned table
blowing a sigh through his
scattered beard,
M. Plato checking his watch
noting Leo's eternal punctuality
deep in his Russian boots
4 o'clock, time for tea
and a lesson in Christian Art.

Still staring at that decadent French
painting are we, Friedrich? What the fuck
can you possibly see
in this perverted sex-affliction?
Tolstoy takes a bite from a raw onion.
Where's Plato? I need my tea.
My dear Friedrich, these so-called
symbolic pictures offer nothing to society
being no more than what they are:
products of a diseased aristocracy;
they teach nothing, say nothing
provide no decent models
to live by; they merely incite (as they
have in you) an unhealthy
nervous agitation.
Look at you! Fixated
by this pagan scene of voluptuous idolatry.
Tears stream down his face
onion juice dribbles his beard
as his teeth sink deep
down through the white
viscous layers.

Nietzsche has heard it all before.
Nonetheless, he must reply:
My dear Count, you know as well as I
why this painting disturbs you.
Because it is not Christian;
in fact it is anti-Christian.

We have before us the Death of Apollo,
the subjugation of Apollonian-Christian
rationality. Twenty centuries of
revisioning the bicameral norm.

In the netherworld of dreams
the forces of passionate intensity,
the cruel, dark gods of intuition
triumph over sick and twisted Reason.

Look! Look how the great God Dionysus
holds captive the feeble Apollo,
how the flesh of the Sun-
God goes gray
and a radiant light
bathes the brow
illuminates the body
of chthonic divinity.

The Duality longs to mate
to propagate
itself in a love-hate relationship.

Does the hand place
or remove the laurel crown?
Is the androgyne a dream of Apollo
or is Apollo become Dion's lap dog?

The whole dilemma of Art
and Life is spelled out for you, my dear Count
but you are too blinded by
Xtian assertions of false morality
to see what is here before you.

A broad sweep of Herr Nietzsche's
hand punctuates his soliloquy,
ending with a fanning
move before his nose
to waft Count Tolstoy's
breath away.

Leo red-faced, half-rising:
Really, Friedrich, you are quite
the fuck impossible, and do stop
calling me "Count," you know
I gave up my title when I freed my serfs.

Plato ambles over to the table
just in time to stop the blows
that glow in both men's eyes,
parts them like a ring-side referee,
Leo's tea balanced on his head,
Nietzsche's schnapps on his elbow,

towel over arm,
placed just so,

2 menus in his teeth
once again
for perfunctory
judicious perusal:

The Menu of M. Plato's Café: A Paracritical Catena
> *Modes of Being*
> *Ideal Forms*
> *Enthousiasmos*
> *Chain of Iron Rings*
> *Socratic Dialogue*

What will it be today, gentlemen?
Tolstoy and Nietzsche confer briefly.
They answer simultaneously:
We'll take the dialogue.
        Very well then.

Plato withdraws a mirror
from the folds of his apron.
           What do I hold in my hand?
A mirror.
           Very true. And what does
           a mirror do?
It reflects the surface
of that which it is held next to.

Plato flips a quarter over his shoulder,
holds up the mirror for rear-
ward view to watch its slow
looping descent
arc across the room
descend just so to the vertical slot
of the Jukebox
of Plato's Café
drop down through
mechanical Newtonian
clockwork guts
to activate A-23:
Bobby Darin's looney croon
emerges from the interstices
of vinyl groove
to rub the smooth walls of the cave
like a tribal cat in heat
with adaptation of Kurt Weil:
blood, knives, sharks and
someone sneaking round a corner
mothers screaming
children oozing life;
in horizontal silvered reflecting-strip

Plato sees a dark form slip
in through the side entrance
below the red glow
of the Exit Only sign
*just a jack-knife
has old McHeath dear* and

Plato lifts an altruistic eyebrow.
Donatien-Alphonse-François,
compte de Sade,
short, pock-marked
lurking in powdered wig,
dressed as a priest
he slides into an empty booth
eyes adjusting to dim light
furtively searching the room
and begins his nightly
soliloquy, baby blue spot
piercing the gloom,
illuminating his
doomed melancholy:

Inside the high
walls of my chateau
enclosed by moat
surrounded by snow
no codes imposed themselves
but those I chose
as I played with my dolls
my toys, blood and sex
mingled with sweat
dripped from my knotted cord
and leather scourge:

Tie Rose to the pillar,
chastisement is mine!

(He pauses to take some wine
from a chalice-shaped flask
hid in his vestments,
wipes his brow and
begins again:

In those golden days of the *Ancien
régime* before Marais' gestapo
Robespierre and prison
I had my little fun
with ladies of every estate:
chains and fetters, rods
dipped in vinegar
brooms and knotted cords
Oh it was lovely
those pretty
welts on actresses' backsides
and the silken cry
of nuns and orphans.

It's not like I was the only
one doing it, you know;
a common amusement then.
I just got caught
and caught
and caught again,
forced to spend
my better years
behind bars
pent up like common
footpad or scum.

Oh I knew you well, Teresa,
wanted you the first time I saw you,
you in your starched white wimple
those upcast pleading eyes
wide in shocked ecstasy

wrapped in a veil of fragility
I wanted that awe for mine own
wanted that pure mouth to moan
in an ecstasy that *I* created.

Jean Genet
in cassock and surplice
enters the same side door
leading Teresa of Avila
blindfolded,
her lovely wrists
behind her back
fastened by silken sash,
her face a mask
of passive ecstasy,
to a café table on the
other side of the room

where he cavalierly
seats her, then crosses
himself as he crosses
back to his waiting master.

Teresa withdraws a small whip
tucked into her ten-decade rosary
that hangs from her cinctured waist
and runs the knotted cords
through her slender fingers.

Donatien leaps to his feet,
eyes shining with anticipation.
Genet plays dutiful altar-boy
reporting to his warden-priest:

"I snatched her just as you said
during the act of communion
a numinous glow
surrounding her face
a halo praying
about her brow
so that I had to drop
a sack on top
her head
to see what I was doing.
All was done as you wished."

The Marquis rubs his hands together
gaily, so rapidly they want to leap into flame,
hesitates, then takes two steps across the floor
to where his angel sits playing with her whip,
the whip she uses each night
while the Marquis watches
with wet lips and liquid eyes.

She deigns to glance up
in his direction, her face a reflection
of all the mysteries in heaven and hell.
They have played this game before
but it never gets any easier:
de Sade's breath catches, his heart
refuses to beat, the beatific
stun of her beauty always makes
him act this way

like a piss-a-bed schoolboy.
He sways and Genet steadies him.

She speaks through milky white teeth
flicking her little whip
gently across the thigh
of her brown and white Carmelite habit:
"Dios mio! Not you two little rascals again!"

Act II

The Eye
demands completeness
in the homogeneity
of isomorphic space.

Time shakes hands with
time, a palsied politician
crippled with hegemony,

wheels his chair
toward some medicine-wheel
of the future where

the four colors
of ultimate direction
meld and mix,

whose curvilinear concerns
are not our own
are not concentric

but shape-shift, streak
like Greek arrows
toward a target unknown.

Michel Foucault,
busboy *extraordinaire*,
shaved pate, eyes a-glare
with what he hopes will be taken as
an intense stare
of POWER

makes his rounds
as he does each night
to sweep the crumbs
from beneath the tables,
to clean and speak
to each ashtray
as if each held some sibylline secret.

Foucault leaps like Nijinsky
high into the air,
hangs there, instantaneously,
a critical parody of being,
his bar-rag poised just so

his domed cranium
a Pan Optical structure seeing
in all directions, probing,
seeking out the soiled
and smudged
detritus
left by
previous
negotiations
with reality,

then floats
down
to the
ground

as if wings
were a common thing
written in
to daily existence.

The Discourse of the Ashtrays

The ashtrays of Plato's Café
are basically of
two types:

1. Those with a heavy base of metallic alloy
   thus insuring their basic intrinsic worth in
   the power structure of mineral hierarchy.

2. Those whose forms are plastic, liminal,
   shape-shifting their malleable forms
   out towards the margins of eternity.

The Mini-Cam of Plato's Café
follows Foucault
on his nightly foray
into dusty syllogism
             dissecting on tape
each move he makes, each play-
by-play repartee
with his trusty rag.

Above the bar we see
the cracked Motorola
TV monitor (black & white) on which the
discourse is broadcast nightly

for the *divertissement* of our doomed
infinite patrons.

Foucault sighs heavily. He's been here before.
The turquoise plastic
1950s futuristic
swept-back tray
at Table 15
      (reserved for Sartre and Robbe-Grillet)
holds only a dried piece
of pink bubble gum and one
fingernail clipping
shaped like a symbol for infinity.

"What do you have to say for yourself,
Number 15?" queries Foucault.
"Undone . . . All totally undone . . . ."

Whoosh! It's gone – swept into Foucault's vacuum
he carries concealed up his sleeve
like a gambler's derringer
he erases what he
does not want to hear,
does not want to feel,
does not want to see

while the Mini-Cam records it all:

      How did it feel, Michel?
          That final terrifying blow
            of power?

Fine, he says, fine, but the
true author has disappeared
from the text, vamoosed
like a cypher
leaked out from the ashes of discourse,
disappeared perhaps up my sleeve,

ask them, ask my little ones.

The Mini-Cam thrusts his mike-
mouth, his slender reticulated metallic throat
into the ashtray's burnt and
gently rippling orifice:

All heads in the Café suspend
their theoretical disbelief:

The Marquis' lips
disengage from Teresa's

Nietzsche's neck
turns from the painting,
even Plato stops
his endless rounds

to hear the ashtray speak:

"Actually, Mike, it was a tough game.
But we were ready,
prepared, you might say
in a way
the examination transformed
the economy of visibility into the
exercise of power."

Foucault winks
to the tray
nods to the cam
and moves on
to the next tableau:

Table 5
a pewter affair
like a sad *chinois* buffet:
3 monkeys perch on the tray
See No, Hear No, Tell No
tales of good or evil, a cigar butt
smashed on blind face
ashes trickle down mute brow
bits of Havana on wrinkled ears:

– the genital form of an apparition
rendered to attend an aperture's Fate –

and the aperture:

Eye
Mouth,
Ear,
Nose,
Anus,
Vulva
       is Power is
a state
of dire straights

of anxiety that is
economically
politically
sexually
self evident
yet cannot compete with thunder

with "Xenophobic Yawning Zeus"
or the phallologocentric
construction of power
in post-millennialist thought.

Act III

Plato jumps down low
like a Caribbean witch doctor
with a jambo in his juju

throws a quarter discus-style
and cracks open
the throat of high celebrity:

a low note of taboo consanguinity
as Bob Marley's slip-slap fills the room:

> *One of these days you gonna hear a voice say RUN*
> *Where you gonna run to?*
> > *Whoa-whoa?*

You gonna run to the Rock and one day
there will be NO ROCK . . .

Sigmund Freud and Lou
enter and stun the room.
Foucault drops an ashtray.

Lou Andreas Salomé,
wide hat cocked
just so
feather boa
kissing her cheek,

looks Nietzsche's way,
her gaze is the gaze
that theorists dream of.

She has, how does one say,
that strong androgynous air
faintly reminiscent of Dietrich
or Sheena, Queen of the Jungle;
she is the Swamp Goddess
of Nietzsche's infernal painting:
you almost expect to see
ferns trail down from her hair,
honeysuckle sprout from her sex.

Plato
does his best stab
at a courtly Viennese bow,
guides them
to the table they died for

and raises one eyebrow:

"Pernod, si'l vous plait,"
says Salomé,
"and a seltzer for the professor."

Her voice is like the tinkling
clink of ice cubes
gone mad
in a half-empty glass
musically full of possibilities
but finite, melting coldly,
oddly away into delirium.

Freud already needs to pee;
he stands up and bows stiffly.
Forgive me, *Liebling*, but I must visit
the "little boy's" room.

Siggy, we just got here
and the first thing you want to do
is stand in front of a toilet.

You know my kidneys are weak, my dear.

It's all in your head, Fred
she says as she watches
his back disappear into gloom.

Nietzsche is ore to her magnet
pulled across the room
to throw himself at her feet
as she sits like an elfin shape
in a Varo painting

a sylph
grinding up stars to spoon-
feed to a caged moon.

Why him and not me, he bleats.

Stop beating yourself, Friedrich,
you are still a small boy
who longs to run away
and join the carnival
while Freud is an industry
whose factories
repeat themselves endlessly
like reifications of desire;

my poor boy,
my poor dear Friedrich,
poor you,
poor us,
as she runs her slender
hands through his hair
and he fills her lap with tears.

Freud is in the men's room
carefully choosing his urinal
slowly unbuttoning
his fly
rehearsing
in his mind's eye
as he does each night
a lecture he gave
long ago:

"His own feces produce no disgust in him;
he values them as part of his own body and is
unwilling to part with them, he uses them as the
first "present" by which he can mark out those people
whom he values especially; his achievements in the way of
urination appear to be the subject of particular pride.

"I know that for some time you have been longing to
interrupt me with cries of "Enough of these monstrosities!
The motions of the bowels a source of pleasurable sexual
satisfaction exploited even by infants! Feces a substance
of great value and the anus a kind of genital organ!
But, I tell you, it is true!"

Freud produces his own
liquid "present" to Plato
in a long steady stream
not without pleasure.

"Idiots! Why should you not know that in many adults,
both homosexual and heterosexual, the anus takes over the
part played by the vagina in sexual intercourse?"

Siggy breaks wind slowly,
flushes the commode
his lecture to the toilets over.

Behind the bar Plato
pours himself a drink
and slowly
eyes the room:

Foucault talking to his ashtrays,
the Marquis and Teresa
making out like high school sweet-
hearts at a Halloween ball
him a priest, her a nun,

Genet scribbling furiously,
Nietzsche weeping at Lou's feet,

Tolstoy asleep,
his onion half-eaten
Freud emerging from the men's room
zipping up his fly.

Plato sighs, inductively,
and shrugs:

Another night
at the café of sorrows,
the café of waking dreams,
of frozen identities.
A slow night for Friday;
on a hot night Sappho
would show with Roland Barthes
and Joan of Arc;
Clarice Lispector
might take tea with Emily Dickinson
or Buddha might waltz in
with Gandhi.

He walks to the Jukebox
and puts another quarter in;
holds up an empty glass
for inspection.

Dance with me, Lou, says Nietzsche
as the first strains of *Begin the Beguine*
filter through the room.

Lou rises lifting Friedrich
to his feet
playing Salomé to his Baptist

> *So then let them begin the beguine;*
> *Let the love that was once a fire*
> *remain an ember . . .*

as Freud appears by their side.

The three embrace,
Siggy and Nietzsche locking arms and hands

Lou fluid, liquidly
caught in the middle

her arms around their
sacrificial necks
as they do a tight
tripartite
tango across the room.

Foucault sprinkles salt on the floor,
Plato smiles and pours
drinks for all.

The Marquis and Teresa
leap to their feet
      in tropical splendor
He whispers into her ear:
"*Mon cher*, you were always my favorite saint."
She kisses his throat and moans:
"And you my favorite monster."

Genet grabs Foucault
and they waltz around the room
their shaved heads making
twin statements of naked obscurity

as the ashtrays sing in unison:
   Oh yes, let them begin the beguine

Tolstoy grabs Plato and they
are all now dancing
dancing
dancing
slowly

around the room
in counter-
clock-wise
movement
faces frozen in
timeless stare
not daring to speak
anymore
not wanting to think
anymore

only driven, propelled
by the same old impulse
that drove their lives
that brought them here:

the Mini-Cam recording it all
swirling images
in black & white
on the cracked Motorola

they watch their
ghostly motions
in shades of gray
swirling, twirling
like lost Vienna
high above the bar

and in the corner,
on the wall,
as the endless curtain
begins to fall,

the Dionysian figure
in Moreau's painting
looms taller now
eyes brighter now
above Apollo;
radiates a strange,
numinous,
phosphorescent glow.

End-Games

The Angel of Time

The Angel of Time follows me,
stalks me down dimly lit corridors,
or on the bright sunny sidewalks
of my small town as I stroll beneath

rolling tumbling clouds the color
of certain cats who duck into
churches whose doors are left open.

Their bells toll in lowsome dirge, each
competing on Sunday; they mourn for the souls of
sinners and praise the smug assurance of the saved.

My Angel of Time (permit me) has purple eyes
rimmed with black; wears lipstick and too much
rouge on his cheeks. He calls himself by the names
of those he seeks, and makes secret forays into
dimensions we can only hope to begin to understand.

My Archangel of Time is often impatient: swings
his flaming sword back and forth like a child's plaything
and longs to sever the strings that anchor me like a circus balloon
floating here alone, so that, cut, I will sail away into the unknown,
unaccompanied, wistfully looked after perhaps
by some dismayed child, but forgotten in a very short while.

To Age Slowly Without Pain

The insubstantial beauty of smoke
lilting upwards from an unseen stack
on a clear winter morning,

lifts the heart as briefly as it rises,
and then fades away with the wind;
attacks the senses with acute demand

as sharp as battle lances brandished
centuries ago in long forgotten China,
where the Confucian texts of war

first were caricatured on slim sticks
of bamboo strung together with silk cords
that crumbled in time, leaving only

confused and jumbled accounts, full
of splintered wisdom about high ground,
bloodless coups, and counter counterspies.

The insubstantial beauty of a sunrise
as it clears the eastern horizon
spreading fingers of golden light

through bare boughs, across frosted roof
tops covering untold joys and sorrows :
nightmares and waking dreams,

forgotten the moment light pales through the window,
never to be recalled until the moment when death
calls, and all forgotten dreams are remembered.

The insubstantial beauty of morning's river,
placid and green, clear and clean, as though
one could walk across its mirrored surface

to the other shore, where the night before
gold and red lights slashed the tide like knives
glittering out to the center, where dreamy boats

flow upstream pushed by the steamy breath
of river spirits, and river gods, who watch us
from the fourth dimension and shed frozen tears

over our ignorant sins, and our transient beauty.
They watch as children wake from fitful sleep
to see air-to-ground missiles explode all around them,

shattering roofs, and walls, and bodies, in their village
sending mushroom clouds of golden fire spiraling upwards
into the black mountain night, beautiful, beautiful

the sight of death who comes roaring down from above
from million dollar flying machines flown by deadly angels,
who are agents of the Dark Star disguised in Christ's apparel.

The insubstantial beauty of life as it morphs into death,
that precise moment when the moth leaves the mouth
and flies to we know not where, to some other dimension

where other frightened children sing one eternal note of dismay,
where bands of white light hum in unison mantras of reckless joy,
forever flying above golden rivers, glowing from endless sunrise.

Two Hundred and Six Bones

The skin that hangs from this skeleton
is cloud stuff: tree limbs on a hilltop
seen from a moving vehicle – ineluctable

like foxfire in nightwind, vanishing within
seconds after sight. The tegument between
these bones feels right; tightened to keep

me strung high and low (*cap a pe*) from waist
to crown to toe and then below all things
connective like my lord's puppet all unstrung.

Femurs found in a dig in Egypt; metatarsals un-
covered beneath centuries of dust in Mesopotamia
and parts of a skull in a helmet in a river in England:

all these things were once living and breathing:
creation's transitive explosion of love
and here I still am in the middle of it all alive

and wondering how it all will end. The thigh
bone connected to the hip bone, the hip bone
connected to the love bone now hear the word

of the Lord. Or is it Darwin? Why must we
choose as if from a menu of entrees in the
bistro of history? Garden of Eden or Olduvai Gorge?

Cain and Abel or Australopithecus africanus?
Noah or Homo erectus? Revelation or walking fish?
Which? Or both, or none? Can anyone judge

or even begin to care? Too many questions
without enough answers. This is the way it
always must be. I can feel it in my bones:

all two hundred and six of them rattling around
in a cage of flesh – bone house, brain house, sea road
of muscle and fat waving us on into infinity's mystery.

Through a Glass Darkly

*Withered willows in the Fall
whither go thy leaves?*

The layers of oversight have been
changed. Bare ruined choirs
stain the landscape dripping with rain

in late November. The 21st century limited
exists in tandem with the 16th and the 1st
when early Christians walked the earth,

were persecuted for forsaking Jupiter
and Roma and Nero the Living God.
The 23rd century is here too with its

impossible robotic perfection swelling
above the iron trees and glass domes
that cover still self-functioning cities :–

emotion sensors in every room to
quickly suss out layers of psychic stress
and oversight with an always watchful

awe-full eye toward change and maxi-fluidity
winking above the intersections of streets
and hallways: Is this not the Ides of March

asks Brutus and Shakespeare writes
this down in his panoptical play that
plays with time simultaneously perceived:

a clock in ancient Rome, chimney tops
above the Tiber (or is it really the Thames?)
and a pulpit for Antony's flaming speech.

In 200 years will mourning doves and
deer searching together for acorns and seeds
seem an anachronism too silly to speak or think,

as silly as Newton's planets still towing the same
old millennial line, elliptical routes gone haywire
the way of the dino and dodo? But they will

(of necessity) still be there by definition in the quantum
merging of past, present, and future all rolled into one jelly
evenly spread on slices of the time-space continuum

likened to a universal loaf of wonder bread
floating in the fifth dimension where you may have
parallel lives as a monk or a nun, a peasant or a czar.

Applications of entanglement have reached
pure states of nonlocality. Newton would have been shocked
off his pedestal and all the sages of antiquity

could not have predicted this spooky turn of events
if one can actually call invisible actions and non-matter current
phenomena. Fie on it! Fie! 'Tis a fardel not worthy to bear.

Science is back once again to magic – or perhaps it never
left it – all is sorcery, all alchemy, voodoo physics
in multi-universe bubble-dome micro and macro expansion :–

Infinity plus one.

Memento Mori

When Death finally comes for me
will she find a malformation in my brain?

A tumor in my soul?
A cave of ice within my heart?

And will she find these things
amiss, normal, or simply banal?

When elegant Death reaches out her
smooth white hand with lace at the wrist

and black-lacquered nails,
will I take it with a courtier's kiss:

an invitation to a marble waltz
on the floor of a Viennese ballroom?

When Death comes knock knock
knocking on my door as if she were

the lyrics to a New Orleans blues song
will I answer like a whore in a bordello

a faded wrap barely concealing my
agèd dishabille? Will she reveal in her chorus

the secret of why I was here, and why
I am now going to wherever she leads me?

Prisoner of Hope

I wake up each morning
amazed that I am still alive.

The weeks keep rolling by
like a large round stone

rolling down a very steep hill
faster and faster gathering

great momentum until
whatever waits at the bottom

shall stop it. Utterly smashing
it to pieces or slowly coming

to a tenuous inertia, settle quite still
and all will be as it once was

in the uttermost beginning, no sight,
no sound, no feeling, simple tranquility.

Song of Gog

And when the thousand years are expired,
Satan shall be loosed out of his prison,
And shall go out and deceive the nations
Which are in the four quarters of the earth,
Gog and Magog, to gather them together to battle:
The number of whom is as the sand of the sea.
      Revelations 20: 7-8

Living in the Land of Gog
we see but dimly
as through scrim of fog.

So much is hidden
from our privy
view, daily we are bidden

to rise up and listen long
to our leaders talk
as they talk through strong

martial voices, intermediaries
on screens chalked
with pie charts and actuaries

whose heads bob and prophesy
war, disaster, horror for
a future we must prepare for by

making sacrifice, keeping ever
vigilant eye out for terror
planned by dark, silent neighbors,

spies of our enemies, the dogs
who live in the Land of Magog
and worship the false god.

Living in the Land of Gog
we must bow to the One God
who knows and sees all: Aygog.

Aygog the All Mighty, who chose
to live among us as common sod
who nightly burned like us and daily froze

and bled Himself for us so that we
lowly might eat and drink of Him,
suffer with Him to make ourselves free

of all that is earthly, all unclean
unseemly habits, unprescribed behavior,
all action not writ down from His dream :

the Great Dream of Aygog that screams
out the aweful name of the Savior
while we are shaken awake, the teaming

multitudes down on their knees
facing the West while the heathen choir
of Magog bow down to the East

and we all chant as one our prayer,
our plea for cleansing war and fire :
for the legions to sweep down where

the forces of Magog gather
and to drown them all in a sea of blood,
a burning sea from the mouth of our Father.

Living in the Land of Gog, we
are lucky to have thinking machines
that do our cleaning, our fighting,

sweep clear the battlefields of bomb
and enemy, sweep our homes clean
from dirt, dust, and sin that come

from the skins of our children
whose lives are fraught and lean
who sweat through the thin

seconds of demand and duty
we must perforce lay upon them
to make them brave and worthy

to run the machines that drop
death upon the heads of the dogs
of Devil-worshipping Magog,

pilotless drones whose eyes
are the fingertips of our offspring
flipping the switch, clicking the keys

that drive our robotic justice over
heathen terrain to do His will,
for we are Aygog's servants forever

and forever will we bend the knee
in duty, in obeisance, vow to kill
all those who, in enmity, follow His enemy

and we greet each morning as the crow
caws gladly his orison shrill,
his prayer to Aygog cleansing his craw,

as the great vulture circles the sky
gliding, ceaselessly watching,
silent of cry, glittering red eye

wide open, dilated nostril breathing
always alert to do Gog's bidding
above the river of Gog, bequeathing

such quietus to morning's gray chill
like a battlefield after the drones
and droids have left it clean and still.

There is a river that flows wide
and long through the Land of Gog,
a river of blood whose high tide

washes up the bodies of those few
who are unholy, unfaithful; traitors who
have not washed themselves in the true

life's blood of He Who Bleeds For All
He Whose Blood is a River:
Aygog, the All-Knowing, vengeful

God of Gog who will destroy
the False God of Magog
like a child who steps on a toy.

And we are all so lucky
living in the Land of Gog
to be democratic and free

unlike the enemy infidel who dwell
in sand beside no cleansing river
whose red tides may dispel

the pall of the mortal curse
by baptism in eternal water.
We sit by these shores and rehearse

the final coming of the Lord
Aygog unto this earth
to free our souls by fiery sword

to raise us up after the final battle
when our killing machines give birth
to Death for our enemies, hot metal

spitting forth righteous grape-shot
and two hundred rounds per second
bi-cameral eye scanning parking lots

and blind alley ways; apartment
hallways, office corridors beckon
them forth to the final judgment,

the bloody reckoning foretold
as it was etched on golden pages
by the gray prophets of old

now in the land of shadow and fog,
the land of shades where holy sages go
after faithfully serving great Aygog :

our reward to see as through scrim
or dark glass the visage grim
of eternity glimpsed through a curtain.

The Psychic Torment of Dreams

A fox calling out at midnight, her high-
pitched cough like a lonely lover's cry.

Telepathic jazz holds back the brute numbness
of the world of logical probability, vocality's mistress

hiding in a dress of distress. It calls out to us
in major changing to minor like a lone coyote

seeking her dead mate or Keats' demon lover
floating on a river of seaweed and sawdust, forever

doomed to wear the mask of Medusa, snakes
of dread locks changing the souls of men to clay,

whisking away young women who become
voluptuous dragonflies in the fairy kingdom

or white butterflies who sing all seasons
in the ever blossoming microcosm of non-reason

to while away the hours betimes with flowers
rare: pink and purple gold and red, violet bowers

that screen from mortal eyes a world seen only
by gods and goddesses the size of ants and snails.

Folly of nightshade's deadly kiss upon lips
that speak while sleeping, eyelids that shutter

and shudder between one world and another
where waking senses hide between sheets of nonsense.

I'll have no more of this but yet I cannot stop it;
it stops me and keeps me stuck like a stopwatch

in some phantom Salvador Dali painting, melting
through my half-awake, half-asleep psychic stress,

broken steps down a crooked staircase, armless embrace,
caress that scares me half to death, half alive with a dreamer's kiss.

*Lines for the End of
the Mayan Calendar*

In dark wet December
five days before winter

body and soul hunger
for light. Gone the sun's

bright apotheosis; healing
catharsis, exchanged like

ill-fitting gifts for gray sky
with naked limbs of oak

and maple stark against it.
This darkness is why

people light up their houses:
drag dead trees inside

and string them up with baubles,
place candles in windows

all to keep the darkness at bay
to chase the fallen angels away

from porch step and doorway.
Night comes too silently now

on stealthy paws, creeping along like
the feral huntress she is, licking

with rough tongue the corners
of rooms, the edges of shadow

until she drops quickly down
on her prey, the remnants of day.

In these mornings and nights
we pray to the master of love and light

the Father-Mother of compassion
to shed his brilliance upon our heads,

our souls. To fill us up with
her radiance, to make us wholly one

with earth, with sky, with the infinite center
of our true existence. Three-part harmony

of body, mind, and soul singing
as one in the vast choir of eternity.

Freedom Day
– Early morning thoughts on July 4th

We hold these truths to be self-evident:
all white men who own property are created equal –
this of course excludes black people and Indian people
and women and poor white whiskey tangos
who have no pot to piss in.

Nonetheless, it is a beautiful morning this morning
when all Americans are freed from work
(except those who work at Walmart and MacDonald's
and Burger King and Pizza Hut and Kroger
and Safeway and Piggly Wiggly)
freed to pursue barbeque picnics by the lake
and drunken relatives
and loud firework displays
that proclaim with colored gunpowder our freedom.

Oh say can you see? Those rockets bursting over your villages
for the past ten years in Iraq and Afghanistan,
the cluster bombs and napalm exploding in jungles
forty years ago in Vietnam, just look at the beautiful tracers
shooting out from the sides of ironic helicopters
bearing the name of those we have subdued –

Apache! Geronimo! shouted those paratroopers
who leaped out of planes on D-Day
two years or so before I was born
into this land of freedom and gory.

The list of those we have invaded to protect our freedom
is too long to tell: hello Philippine Islands, hello Nicaragua,
Guatemala, Panama, Grenada, Cuba, Tunisia, Libya,
Iraq, Afghanistan, Vietnam, Laos, Cambodia,
Japan (and all the islands she laid claim to)
Germany, Italy, Mexico, the Korean Peninsula,
the Five Nations, the Creek Nations, the Cherokee Nation,
the Chickasaw Nation, the Shawnee Nation, the Sioux Nations,
the Comanche Nations, the Yuma, the Pomo, the Ute,
the Cheyenne, Blackfoot, Crow, the Mandan, the Sauk and Fox,
the Navajo, the Hopi, Apache, Pueblo, all those half naked
starving savages we small-poxed and grape-shot out of existence
and gave the remaining few their freedom on reservations
in Oklahoma where the wind comes whippin' cross the plains,
freedom to be Americans just like you and me.

Gun

Oh America,
you never got over your youth –

All those slap-happy penny dreadful
tales of Billy the Kid & Wild Bill H.

went to your head and stayed there
like lead poisoning. You talkin' to me?

You must be talkin to me cause they
ain't nobody else – Draw! And two

Lone Star College students shoot it out
in the O.K. Cafeteria letting some air into

each other and plugging a janitor who
got in de way.

Oh America,
what teenage boyhood fantasies

roll round in yo' empty head. Bang Bang
yer dead. Yer one dead injun and I'm

the rootin-tootin cowboy on this block
with my cap gun and my Glock.

Fandango

The last few bars of Mysticali Rose
drifting down the street
mixt with dust and rolling mesquite
the beat lingering there
in that corner where
heat gathers itself up into a knot
of tangled memories and squats
in a heap of rags and print
and sighs out loud for squandered love.

You want to sing
but cannot even hum.
You want to scream
but no sound escapes your mouth.

Only the white moth flies out
making good her fatal break
as bone men strum their liquid guitars
and proud dancers in red shake
their fiery heads in tune, in tune
with the fierce rhythms of leaving.

Poem at the End of a Deadly Year

Closing in on the end of the year,
Night falling. Dusk settles like gray ash
In a black wood stove as big as the universe
And I hear the cries of help, the burning cries of love

Echoing on the hills of this valley, the bank-plains
Swallowed whole by the mouth of the tide
That takes in all, gives back all, eventually.
The river moves toward the new year relentlessly,

As she must, as she does each cycle of the earth's
Revolution. My sister trees bend with the wind's
Instruction. They rebel not. They conform not,
They simply do. Do the will of her command as

Heavy clouds scud past them eastward, they
Blow westward toward the setting sun,
Their black limbs a fractal repetition of the endless pattern,
The ultimate will of uncertainty and a sure claim

For futurity. For the indecision of our lives.
The sky purples as the lights come on in the town below.
The Shaman Tree keeps watch, her full crown green and blowing
Like saxophone dreams of yesterday and tomorrow,

Forever glowing in red heat like a child's heart at Christmas
Not looking for the born messiah but eager for presents.
Eager for hope blown from a horn not of this world
And the end of all this eager dreaming is this:

A promise. A wish fulfilled. That we might live
So that we might die in such a way that we might live
Again. Again and again or else eternally in some other guise
Some other alter-ego-ness not Freudian or Jungian

Or Christian Noel Oh Hear the Angel Voices,
But another promise, another eager wish fulfilled:
That of nature's light come to surround all existence,
Come to shawl and shroud the precise persistence of love.

Gabriel's Horn

Of the coming of the conurbation of the planet
this much can be said:
                     knuckle down and buckle in
cause it's gonna be a bumpy ride
as the sundry clash of Kalashnikovs

already is heard throughout the continents.

The black crow
like a minstrel showgirl
laughs in my face
with a baby's cry and I enjoy the embrace
of a faded outworn destiny.

Desideratum

Dug deep like a plowed field
unplanted, lacking the green truth
of growth,

three furrows now
mark the smooth brow
of youth.

The seven powers of wrath
buried deep within
my soul

come to me at night
in dreams where I strike out
at strangers

woken by the physical act
of pounding the mattress
or fighting the very air:

acts of rage that boil
up to the surface unbidden
and untaught,

unheard of in day to day
conscious thought
fraught with anxiety

knuckles bloody
from hitting the wall
in my sleep. How

deep is this wrath
dug into my soul?
Where does it go when

dawn comes and lifts
me to another world,
another dimension?

Am I normal (what then *is* normal?),
sane as any other human creature?
Or have my wits vanished in sleep?

What fires together wires together
the clichéd pundits say. Are we tethered
to each other through neural networks

we have no control over, or forked
paths that never cross until the edge
of the mega-multi-verse where all things

come together in a crossing
of parallel lines like some
gigantic railway accident waiting

to happen in the far reaches
of bubble-dome space curved back
upon itself like Möbius's fabled strip

or Captain Kirk's final LSD trip
on the Ur-planet of Hippies
deep in unreachable hyper-space?

Is this the place we dreamed of
in our youth where all our loved ones
will be together forever singing

the same haunted tune
our forefathers sang at the altars
of ritual doom? The gloomy old

rooms of antiquity borderless
in non-Euclidean space bereft
of fusty relatives and dusty ancestors

who wore out their welcomes
decades ago like overstuffed
horsehide chairs or cracked marble mantles.

Wrath buried deep beneath
catholic soul and electromagnetic sensors;
anger forced down into the nightmare time:

Listen to me: I have something to
tell thee: I love . . . what? Myself,
you, all of humanity, saints, sinners,

victims, floods, earthquakes, spring in
all her grandeur, the summer's umber
heat – the winter's grim grin frozen

like a daiquiri or goldfish in a shallow
pond in late December. I love . . . what?
Christ? St. Cecilia? Mother Mary, Mother

Earth, Money? Poetry? Dogs, cats, rabbits,
foxes, turtles, wolves, deer, and all the flowers
that sing in spring and bloom all year :

autumn's fragile memory
caught in the mystery-grip of tears
shed for one's inescapable slide into dying

while still living the past of grade-
school chums who bullied you and
loved you; your first high-school sweet-

heart buried deep down in your psyche
with sister-and-mother-and father's Freudian
baggage strapped to your back

like a monkey on your soul, like a hack-
saw cutting through your heart's
awkward chambers, coronary coronas

like a crown of thorns wrapped tight
around pulsing muscle on the holy-card visions
of my youth. I live; I dream; I love . . . what?

Touch and timbrel, sight and sound
synthesized percussion of small white wings
flying above five-foot Easter Lilies

swaying pink in the breeze that lifts my hair,
that wafts the willow limbs, that combs
out the clover tips mixt with grass on the lawn

aching with life and death here at the juncture
of earth and air, heaven and hell, today
and tomorrow which is always knowingly now.

Curry my soul with a brush
made of meadow. Harrow my heart
with a hoe made of fire that glows

in the dark night like a night-light
showing the way to safety and salvation.
Lead the way, eternal angel, I am ready.

Eavesdropping in Plato's Café is a collection of lyrical, elegiac, and dramatic poems that are at once philosophical and personal, encompassing the broad sweep of history from ancient Greece to post-millennial America. The title poem and others in the collection touch on the intellectual and aesthetic history of the West, while others trace a highly personal spiritual evolution incorporating both eastern and western spiritual thought. The poems, both the long ones and the shorter lyrics, are filtered through an understanding that we as human beings are all temporal creatures striving toward some understanding of why we are here and where we are going. They speak through a highly charged musical idiom that touches the intellect as well as the heart.

Jack Ramey

www.ingramcontent.com/pod-product-compliance
Lightning Source LLC
Chambersburg PA
CBHW021442080526
44588CB00009B/652